W9-AIA-143

9/03

27.07

The Life of Plants

Plant Classification

Richard & Louise Spilsbury

Heinemann Library
Chicago, Illinois

Customer Service 888-454-2279
Visit our website at www.heinemannlibrary.com

Designed by Macwiz
Illustrated by Jeff Edwards
Originated by Ambassador Litho Ltd
Printed by Wing King Tong, Hong Kong

07 06 05 04 03
10 9 8 7 6 5 4 3 2 1

Library of Congress Cataloging-in-Publication Data
Spilsbury, Richard, 1963-
  Plant classification / Richard and Louise Spilsbury.
     v. cm. -- (Life of plants)
Includes bibliographical references (p.   ).
Contents: What is classification? -- Name calling -- The kingdoms of
life -- Within the plant kingdom -- What are algae? -- Types of algae --
Mosses and liverworts? -- Types of mosses and liverworts -- Ferns,
horsetails and clubmosses -- Types of ferns -- What are conifers? --
Types of conifers -- What are flowering plants? -- Classifying flowering
plants -- Types of flowering plants -- Why are flowering plants
successful? -- Plants: then and now -- Studying plants -- Try it
yourself! -- Looking at plant classification.
  ISBN 1-4034-0293-0 (HC)   1-4034-0501-8 (PB)
  1. Plants--Juvenile literature. 2. Botany--Classification--Juvenile
literature. [1. Plants. 2. Botany--Classification.] I. Spilsbury,
Louise. II. Title.
  QK49 .S74 2002
  580--dc21
                        2001008299

Acknowledgments
The author and publishers are grateful to the following for permission to reproduce copyright material: pp. 4, 7, 8, 13, 16, 19, 20, 21, 22, 23, 25, 28, 32, 33, 39 Holt Studios; pp. 5, 6, 14, 15, 24, 34, 37 Corbis; pp. 10, 31 FLPA; pp. 12, 17, 18, 26, 27, 30, 35, 38 Oxford Scientific Films; p. 29 Photodisc; p. 36 Science Photo Library; flower motif Hemera.
Cover photographs reproduced with permission of A-Z Botanical Collection Ltd, Holt Studios, Natural Visions.

Some words are shown in bold, **like this.** You can find out what they mean by looking in the glossary.

Contents

A plant may be called different things in different countries, so every type of plant has a Latin name that can be recognized anywhere in the world. Latin names are made of two words—the first is the **genus,** or general, group a plant belongs to and the second is its **species,** or specific, name. Latin plant names are given in brackets throughout this book.

What Is Classification?

Ever since humans first walked the Earth, they have tried to make sense of their surroundings. With so many different plants and animals, it helps to be able to recognize and name them. But it is also helpful to understand how each one is similar to another one. This is what classification is all about—grouping living things according to the characteristics they share.

Sometimes the similarities among **organisms** are many. For example, all elephants are large and gray and have a trunk. All of them clearly belong to the same group. Other times, similarities are few. An elephant and a daisy clearly belong to different groups.

◄ When we classify a tree as an oak, we are not just describing its leaf shape and acorns. We also are saying that it belongs to the same group as all other oak trees.

Ancestors

If you have red hair, it is probably because your parents or **ancestors** had red hair. Many plants have common features because they share ancestors. All the plants on Earth today have ancestors that first existed millions of years ago. So, an important part of classification is the story of the past.

History of classification

The first humans on Earth probably classified plants as good or bad to eat and animals as safe or dangerous to approach. Information such as this would have been very important to them. People needed to know which animals they could hunt and which might hunt them; which berries they could eat safely and which might poison them. This helped them to find food. They also may have grouped organisms according to shape or color.

From Aristotle to Linnaeus

The ancient Greek thinker Aristotle lived more than 2,000 years ago. He was important in the history of classification because he figured out the main differences among animals and plants. Back then we knew of only a thousand or so different types of organisms. Centuries of study and observation followed in which other scientists from many countries classified more and more organisms.

By figuring out similarities and differences among living things, they could also divide them into groups. In the 1700s, Swedish scientist Carl von Linné (Linnaeus) figured out a way to classify organisms. His system is the basis for the one used around the world today.

◄ Carl von Linné was known throughout the world as Linnaeus.

Name Calling

Today, as in Linnaeus's time, there are many different names for the same plants in different countries. What is called a daisy in England is called a *margherita* in Italy. In the past, when people spoke or wrote to each other about plants, they often got confused.

Linnaeus's double-name system

To solve this problem, Linnaeus decided that each plant or animal should have a double name that could be used all over the world. He chose to write these double names in Latin, since that was a language understood in most countries at the time.

In this double name system, the first name is the **genus,** or general group, to which the plant or animal belongs. The second name describes the **species,** or specific group. For example, the English daisy is *Bellis perennis*. *Bellis* tells us the genus to which this daisy belongs. Other plants with similar features also have this same first name. *Perennis* is the species name. Only plants and animals of the same species can **reproduce** together. So only two daisies of the same species can successfully breed together in the wild.

◄ **The genus name for maple is *Acer*. There are about 200 trees and shrubs in the *Acer* genus. Each has its own species name. Red maple is also named *Acer rubrum*.**

Names with a story to tell

The names in Linnaeus's system often say something about the way a plant looks or grows. For example, *Campanula* means "bell-shaped" in Latin. It is the name for a genus of plants with bell-shaped flowers. The Latin name for spiked bellflower is *Campanula spicata*. *Spicata* means "spiked." The bearded bellflower is also in the genus *Campanula*, but it has the species name *barbata*, which means "bearded."

Clovers usually have three leaves. They belong to the genus *Trifolium*. *Tri* means "three," and *folium* means "leaf."

It can be fun to guess what plant names mean. For example, *odorata* means the plant has a smell or odor. *Splendifera* means the plant is splendid, or showy.

Most of us still use common names when we talk about plants. However, it is good to know there is a universal naming system we can use to avoid confusion.

▲ The bearded bellflower has the Latin name *Campanula barbata*.

Naming today

Today scientists use special equipment to compare the **genes** of organisms. This helps them to classify both plants and animals. When scientists find a new species, large international committees must check to be sure that it really is new and then decide on a new name for it.

The Kingdoms of Life

Giving an **organism** a name that distinguishes it from all other organisms is one part of classification. To make even more sense of life on Earth, it is useful to group organisms that have certain things in common. These things may have to do with the way the organisms **reproduce,** how they feed, or what's inside their **cells.**

All organisms can be divided into five large groups called **kingdoms.** The organisms in one kingdom are more similar to each other than they are to organisms in the other kingdoms. Plants and animals are the best known of these kingdoms.

Plant producers

Take a look at a tree and then at yourself. It is pretty obvious how you differ from a tree! You can move. It cannot. You have arms and legs. It has a trunk and branches. However, the single most remarkable thing that distinguishes plants from other living things is that they produce their own food inside their bodies. They do this through the process of **photosynthesis.** Plants use the energy produced through photosynthesis to change water and **carbon dioxide** into sugars and **oxygen.**

▲ Plants are called **producers** because they produce their own food. Photosynthesis takes place in their leaves.

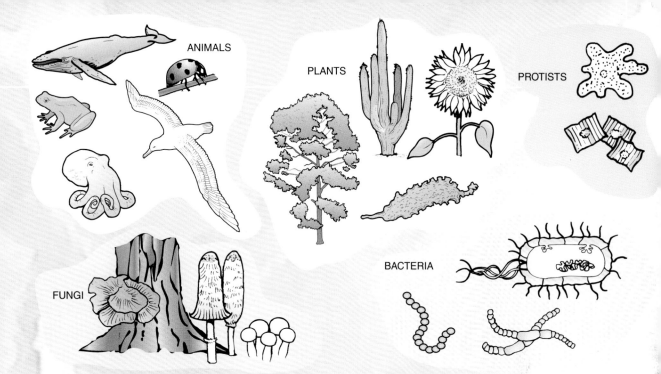

ANIMALS

PLANTS

PROTISTS

FUNGI

BACTERIA

▲ These are the five kingdoms of life.

Animal consumers

All animals need to eat food to survive. Animals cannot make their own food like plants can. Animals are **consumers.** They consume, or eat, plants or other animals that eat plants. This means that plants, either directly or indirectly, are the source of all food animals need to survive.

The other three kingdoms

All other living things on Earth that are not plants or animals make up the three other kingdoms. Many **fungi** may look like plants, but they belong in a separate kingdom. The fungi include organisms such as mushrooms and toadstools.

The other two kingdoms are made up of organisms you can see only through a microscope. They are single cells or groups of identical cells joined together. **Bacteria** are found in the air, soil, and water. **Protists** live in water and form sea **plankton.**

Expanding kingdoms

So far, more than 1.75 million different **species** have been identified. More are discovered all the time. It is unlikely that we will find many new large animals or plants. However, there are probably many undiscovered insects, bacteria, and protists. The total number of different species could be close to 13 million!

Within the Plant Kingdom

The plant **kingdom** contains **organisms** as different as mosses and cacti. It is useful to divide the plant kingdom into smaller groups that have certain things in common. This helps us study and discuss them. One way to group plants is by how they take in water and **nutrients**—that is, whether they are **vascular** or **nonvascular**.

▲ A vascular plant such as this bamboo can grow tall. Its vessels carry the water it needs from its roots to its leaves many feet away.

Vascular plants

The majority of plants on Earth are vascular. They have vessels, or tubes, inside their **roots, stems,** and leaves. These vessels are connected like the network of pipes in your home that brings water to your sink or bathtub. Some vessels in vascular plants carry water and nutrients from the roots to the other parts of the plant. These vessels are called **xylem.** Other tubes carry sugar made in the leaves by **photosynthesis.** These vessels are called **phloem.**

Nonvascular plants

Nonvascular plants do not have vessels to transport water and nutrients. They tend to live in damp places near the ground. Here all parts of their bodies can absorb, or take in, what they need. Therefore, nonvascular plants rarely grow as tall as vascular plants do.

Plant divisions

The world of plants is usually divided into five smaller groups or divisions. Members of each division **reproduce** in a similar way or have similar structures. For instance, plants are put in one division or another depending on whether or not they reproduce using **seeds** or whether their seeds grow in **cones** or flowers.

Two divisions contain nonvascular plants. The first is algae, which includes water plants such as kelp. The second is mosses and liverworts, which are small green plants that live in damp places.

The three remaining divisions contain vascular plants. One is ferns and their relatives. Club mosses and horsetails are grouped with ferns because, although they don't resemble ferns, they have a lot in common with them. The second vascular division is the conifers, which contains plants such as fir, pine, and redwood. Conifers bear their seeds in cones. Conifers are grouped with their close relatives, the cycads and ginkgoes. The final vascular division is flowering plants. Although their variety in shape and size is astonishing, flowering plant **species** are grouped together because they all reproduce using flowers.

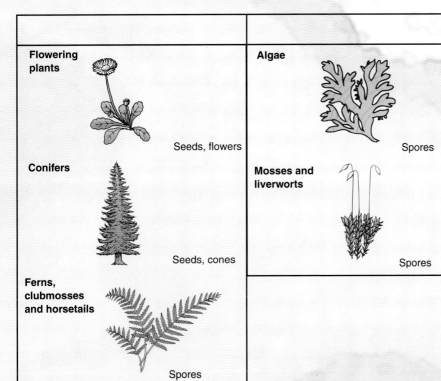

Flowering plants

Seeds, flowers

Conifers

Seeds, cones

Ferns, clubmosses and horsetails

Spores

Algae

Spores

Mosses and liverworts

Spores

◄ The plant kingdom is divided into five groups. There are more flowering plants on Earth than any other kind of plant. Nine out of ten of all plant species are flowering plants.

What Are Algae?

Algae are thought to be the **ancestors** of all land plants. Algae are often described as simple plants. Some are made up of only one **cell** or several very similar cells in a chain or thread. Other larger types have large leaf-like **fronds.** Some algae can be seen only under a microscope. Others can grow to many feet in length.

Algae are **nonvascular** plants and do not have leaves, **stems,** or **roots.** All algae live in water or in moist places, where any part of their bodies can absorb, or take in, what they need. Living in water also helps algae to keep their shape. Fronds and threads float in water, often with the help of built-in water wings. This allows each part of the plant to absorb the sunlight it needs for **photosynthesis.**

▲ The water that algae grow in provides support and most of what they need to make their own food.

Slip and slide

If you have ever walked on a beach at low tide you may have noticed how rocks covered in seaweed are slippery. This is because seaweed—algae that live in or by the sea—are covered in slime. Many algae out of water can lose water through **evaporation.** To help prevent water loss, algae make slime. This forms a second skin on their fronds.

Overactive algae

Single-celled algae **reproduce** very quickly where there are extra nutrients in the water, often as a result of **pollution**. These gigantic increases in population are called algal blooms. The blooms use up a lot of the **oxygen** in the water. Animals and other plants in the water then die because they cannot survive without oxygen.

Algae do not need roots. All their parts absorb the **nutrients** they need from the water they live in. However, many seaweeds need to grow on particular parts of the seashore so that rough waves or strong sunlight cannot damage them. For this reason, they grow **holdfasts** or suckers, which often look like roots, to grip the rocks.

New algae

The simplest, single-celled algae produce new algae by dividing into two identical cells. Larger algae produce **spores**. The spores form inside special areas on the fronds. Some spores have very tough skins that protect the cells inside from cold, heat, and **drought.** In the right conditions, often when the water gets warmer, the cells in each spore may divide and grow into a new, microscopic plant. The new plant produces male or female **sex cells.** If these are brought together by movements in the water, the **fertilized** female cell grows into a new spore-producing plant.

Types of Algae

Ask someone to name a type of algae, and he or she will likely say seaweed. However, there are actually about 12,000 different **species** of algae. Only about half of them live in the sea.

Algae come in many colors: yellow-green, golden-brown, green, brown, and red. Most green algae live in or around the edges of ponds and lakes. Some live in seawater. Still others live on land or on damp surfaces such as old metal gates. In South America, tiny green algae live on slow-moving three-toed sloths. This gives the sloth a greenish tinge that helps it hide in the trees! Green algae are often delicate plants, one or a few **cells** across. However, one very familiar type, sea lettuce, can be 12 inches (30 centimeters) long.

◄ These tiny algae float in the sea. They are called phytoplankton.

Living in harmony

Lichen are **organisms** that look like plants, but they are actually a partnership of algae and **fungi**. Each type of organism needs the other to live. The algae make sugar by photosynthesis to feed themselves and the fungi. In turn, the fungi shelter and collect water for the algae. The two organisms grow together and are so closely entwined that scientists gave them their own separate name—lichen.

The colors of algae

Seaweeds are usually classified according to the colors in their cells. Different colored seaweeds live in different places in the sea.

Algae contain the green substance **chlorophyll,** so they can make food by **photosynthesis.** However, little sunlight reaches deeper water. Green seaweeds are more familiar to us because they grow in shallow water. Red and brown algae have special colors that help them make food with less light.

Red algae live mostly in deep seawater in warm parts of the world. However, some live in shallow rock pools, forming white crusts around the edges of the pools. The largest and toughest algae on Earth are brown algae. Some, such as bladderwrack, have air-filled bladders, or bubbles, on their **fronds** that help them float.

▲ Giant brown kelp grows up to 197 feet (60 meters) long in the cool waters off California. It forms vast underwater forests.

Algae—the key to ocean life

There would be no life in the ocean without algae. Tiny animals eat the billions of tiny single-celled algae that float at sea. Small fish and shrimp eat these animals. Then they become food for larger animals such as big fish, birds, and seals.

What Are Mosses and Liverworts?

Have you ever looked at the tiny plants that grow on damp walls and roofs, on rocks near waterfalls or streams, or on fallen trees in the woods? Among other things, you may have seen green, cushion-shaped plants that feel like sponges if you touch them gently. These are **colonies** of hundreds or even thousands of tiny moss plants. You may also have seen small, flat green plants that look like mini-seaweed. These are liverworts.

▲ Moss plants usually live in colonies, like this. Each plant is sheltered better this way than it would be if it grew on its own. Also, the gaps between each plant in the colony can store more water.

Mosses and liverworts are **nonvascular** plants. They make their own food inside their leaves by **photosynthesis.** However, they do not have **phloem** to carry food to their different parts. Like algae, they generally live in damp places, so their parts can get water and **nutrients** from their surroundings.

Mosses have small, pointed leaves arranged in spirals around their **stems.** Their leaves are not waxy like those of some plants. This means they tend to dry out quickly in the wind or sun due to **evaporation.** Some mosses have hollow **cells** that can soak up water. This allows the plant to save water for dry conditions.

Reproduction

Both mosses and liverworts **reproduce** using **spores.** You may have seen little **stalks** with lumps at the end growing out of moss cushions. The lumps are called **capsules,** which are special boxes that make spores. Moss capsules often have jagged openings called teeth. These teeth can open when the air is dry and close when it is damp. Spores blow from a capsule when the teeth are open.

If a moss or liverwort spore falls onto damp ground, it can **germinate** and grow into a new plant. The new plant grows female and male parts that produce **sex cells.** If there is enough water around the plants, the male sex cells from one moss plant can swim to the female sex cells on another. If a female sex cell is **fertilized** by a male sex cell, it begins to grow into a new spore capsule.

Some flat liverworts have tiny cups on the top of their leaves. Each cup develops bud-like parts inside. Each of these parts can grow into another liverwort plant identical to its parent.

▼ Liverwort capsules often look like tiny flowers. Special dead cells in the capsule twist and snap as they dry. This flicks the spores out. This liverwort is called *Pellia.*

Types of Mosses and Liverworts

At first glance, most mosses look alike. Remarkably, however, there are about 10,000 **species** of moss in the world! Mosses range in size from the three-foot-long (one-meter-long) Brook moss to tiny plants best seen under a magnifying glass. Most are less than four inches (ten centimeters) high. The easiest way to tell mosses apart is by the arrangement of their leaves or the shape of their **capsules.**

Pollution patrol

Mosses are more sensitive to air **pollution** than other plants are. This means they are the first to disappear from a habitat when pollution levels begin to rise. This is why mosses can help tell us about the amount of pollution in the air.

▲ If all the sphagnum moss colonies in the world were put together, they would cover an area half the size of the United States.

Where do mosses grow?

Mosses usually grow in damp, sheltered places on the ground or on trees. However, some are found in more extreme conditions, from hot **rain forests** to freezing Arctic **tundra.** Because many moss species only grow in certain **habitats,** they can give us clues about the soil or rock they are growing on. Sphagnum moss is the name given to several moss species, some green and some red. Sphagnum moss usually grows in cool, wet places called bogs. They grow in **colonies**—some of them massive—around the world.

As sphagnum moss and other bog plants die, they rot slowly in the bog water. Eventually they form a thick sludge at the bottom of the bog. Over long periods of time, more and more plants die, and the sludge forms a dense soil called **peat.** People grow plants on peat, as it is full of **nutrients.** Peat is also cut into blocks, dried out, and burned as fuel.

Liverworts

There are about 7,000 species of liverwort on Earth. They almost always grow in very damp places. However, some prefer hot conditions while others prefer cool conditions. Around half of all liverwort species are flat, single leaves held to the ground by rootlets, or small **roots.** The rest look a lot like mosses. After a forest fire, liverwort **spores** often **germinate** and form large colonies very quickly.

▲ **Liverwort leaves have a liver shape.**

Using mosses and liverworts as medicine

Sphagnum moss soaks up liquids quite quickly. During World War I, soldiers and doctors sometimes used moss to dress, or cover, wounds. This is because the moss successfully soaked up blood.

Liverworts were given their name because their leaves are shaped like the human liver. In the past, some people mistakenly believed that a plant's shape was a clue to how it could be used as medicine. So liverwort was used to treat liver illnesses—without any success!

Ferns, Horsetails, and Club Mosses

Ferns are the largest part of one division of the plant **kingdom.** But this division also includes their relatives, the club mosses and horsetails. These plants look different from ferns, but they have a lot in common with them.

Fern reproduction

Ferns **reproduce** using **spores.** Fern spores are made in cases called **sporangia.** These usually form brown patches on the underside of **fronds.** When spores are ripe, they are released and blow away from the parent plant. If a spore **germinates,** it does not grow into a new fern right away. First, it grows into a tiny green plant-like flap called a **prothallus.** Its job is to produce female and male **sex cells.** Then, in the damp undergrowth, water washes a male sex cell onto a female sex cell. When the **cells** join, a new fern plant begins to grow. When the new plant has **roots** and leaves of its own, the prothallus dies.

▶ The brown patches on the back of this fern frond are sporangia.

Leaves, stems, and roots

All plants in the fern division are **vascular.** They have **stems** and roots, which carry water, **nutrients,** and sugar. Fern fronds contain **veins** that connect with the vessels inside the stems and roots. Club mosses may look like mosses, but like ferns and unlike mosses, they are vascular. Horsetail stems are hollow, and the vessels inside the stems are arranged around the edge. Horsetails have no fronds. Instead, they have rings of short branches like soft needles along the stem.

Most ferns have special underground parts called **rhizomes.** Rhizomes look like roots, but they are stems from which roots and shoots grow. In the winter, fern fronds die. But rhizomes store food that can be used to release **energy** to grow new leaves in the spring. Horsetail stems also grow out of rhizomes. Some horsetail stems are green and branched. Others are brown and straight.

▶ **Some horsetail stems have swollen ends like very soft cones. These are the sporangia, where spores are made.**

Wanted—dead or alive

The resurrection plant (*Selaginella lepidophylla*) is a type of club moss that lives in places with long seasons of **drought**. At these times when water is scarce, the plant curls into a tight, brown ball. Most people would believe the plant is dead. When rain falls, the plant miraculously comes back to life, uncurling its leaves, which then turn green.

Types of Ferns

There are about 12,500 different **species** of ferns on Earth. They range in size from tiny plants less than an inch (three centimeters) long, such as mosquito fern (*Azolla*), that float on water, to tree ferns up to 66 feet (20 meters) tall in **rain forests.**

▲ On a woodland floor, the first sign of a fern is a strange, green curl that looks like the spiral top of a violin. This is a frond growing up toward the light. As the frond grows, it will uncurl and open into a long, feathery shape.

Different fern species often have names that describe their **frond** shape. American Hart's tongue fern (*Asplenium scolopendrium*) has straight-edged fronds that look like an adult male deer's tongue, which is called a hart. The fronds of the shuttlecock fern (*Matteuccia struthiopteris*) are divided into long central **stalks** with many leaflets, or tiny leaves, arranged down their edges. Each frond looks like a giant feather, so the fern plant looks like the shuttlecock used to play badminton! On the northern maidenhair fern (*Adiantum*), the **veins** in the leaflets look like a young lady's long, straight hair.

Tree ferns

There are thousands of tree fern species (*Cyathea*). Many live in Australia and New Zealand. The stalks of their fronds grow together to form a tall, thick, hard trunk similar to a palm tree's trunk. The Cooper's cyathea tree fern's (*Cyathea cooperi*) trunk can grow up to 49 feet (15 meters) tall with fronds up to 20 feet (6 meters) long. Scars on the trunk show where old leaves once grew. **Roots** grow down the sides of the trunk and into the ground for support.

Fern features

Different types of ferns have different shaped patches of **sporangia.** Some people mistake these for signs of disease. Sometimes the sporangia are arranged in lines of dots or streaks along each frond, as in the American Hart's tongue fern. But sometimes the sporangia are around the edge of each leaflet, as in the brackenfern (*Pteridium aquilinum*). Royal ferns (*Osmunda regalis*) have sporangia on separate fronds.

Most ferns live in damp soil, but some find the growing conditions they need on other plants. Most staghorn ferns (*Platycerium bifurcatum*) are **epiphytes.** Their **spores** can **germinate** and grow on bark high up in rain forest trees. Bracken can do well in dry places because it can spread by using its underground **rhizomes.**

Types of horsetails and club mosses

There are about 30 horsetail and 400 club moss species on Earth. The largest are around 10 feet (3 meters) high, but most are less than 12 inches (30 centimeters) tall. Most grow in wet places. Some thrive on ground that contains few **nutrients.** Horsetails and club mosses are found around the world. However, club mosses are more common in **tropical** countries.

Hard-working horsetail

The scouring rush (*Equisetum hyemale*) is a type of horsetail. It makes large amounts of a sharp crystal called silica in its **stems.** In parts of Mexico, bunches of scouring rush are used like sandpaper for polishing wood.

▼ Some club mosses, like this *Lycopodium*, have stiff and prickly stems.

What Are Conifers?

Conifers are trees and shrubs that grow woody or scaly **cones**. Unlike algae, mosses, liverworts, and ferns—which all **reproduce** using **spores**—conifers reproduce using **seeds**. Cones contain and protect the seeds as they develop.

Cones versus flowers

Female cones have the same job as flowers do. They both make seeds. But seeds made by a flower form inside a **fruit,** while conifer seeds do not. A few conifers, such as juniper, have brightly colored cones shaped like berries. This attracts animals that eat the flesh and drop the seeds away from the parent plant.

Conifers actually have two different types of cones—male and female. Male cones are usually small, and they make a dust called **pollen**. Each pollen grain contains male **sex cells**. Female cones are larger and contain female sex cells. In dry weather, breezes blow pollen from male cones onto female cones. If a male cell **fertilizes** a female cell, an **embryo** will grow inside a seed. Seeds also contain a small food supply that the embryo uses to **germinate**. When the seeds are ready, the cones fall or open up to release them.

▼ The female cones on a Douglas fir are reddish and look like flowers. The male cones are yellow and droopy.

Leaves and trunks

The leaves of most conifers are shaped like needles. Some have scale leaves that are shaped like the scales on a fish. Their narrow shape and a waxy coating help keep conifers from losing water through **evaporation.** This means they can survive in places that do not provide enough rainfall for broad-leafed trees. Most conifers are **evergreen.** When a conifer's leaf dies, it drops from the tree. But conifers do not shed their leaves all at once as **deciduous** trees do.

Conifers are **vascular** plants. As they grow bigger, they make extra **xylem** vessels with tough, thick walls. This is called wood. Tough woody trunks give conifers the strength to grow to massive sizes.

▲ Many conifers, like this pine tree, have a special sticky **sap** called **resin** in their trunks. Here, sap is being collected in pans.

Cycads and ginkgoes

Conifers have two close relatives that look quite different from them but also make their seeds in cones. Cycads are evergreen trees. Most look like a cross between a tree fern and a palm tree. Some have brightly colored seeds and rely on beetles to carry their pollen. Ginkgoes are deciduous and have unusual fan-shaped leaves. They can grow up to 99 feet (30 meters) tall. Ginkgo seeds look like yellow cherries.

Types of Conifers

Many conifers are familiar trees in gardens, parks, and forests. Some people bring conifers into their homes to celebrate Christmas. Conifers often can be identified by their distinctive shapes, bark, **cones,** and needles.

The pine family

Of the 500 different **species** of conifers, over half belong to the pine family. This includes the pines but also the firs (*Abies*), cedars (*Cedrus*), spruces (*Picea*), and larches (*Larix*). Most grow in cold, often mountainous places in northern parts of the United States, Europe, and Asia.

Many spruces and firs grow into large trees in just a few years. This is why they are often grown for **timber.** However, some pines grow very slowly and can live to old ages. In pines and spruces, female cones are often woody, brown, and long. In cedars and firs, female cones are shaped like eggs. Pine needles are usually long, narrow, and clustered in groups. They contain **resin,** giving them a nice smell.

The secret of eternal youth?

Some bristlecone pines (*Pinus longaeva*) in California are nearly 5,000 years old. So what is their secret? They have very hard, resin-filled wood that cannot be invaded by bugs. The cold, dry air in the mountains where they live also helps preserve them. Although large parts of their trunks die if they are struck by lightning or damaged, tiny strips of living bark can keep them going. Some leaves stay on the trees for up to 45 years.

Southern conifers

The Chile pine (*Araucaria*) and podocarpus trees of South America, southern Africa, and New Zealand look much different than other conifers. Monkey puzzle trees have flat, leathery leaves with sharp points that often grow in spirals along their branches. They also have spiky cones that look like tiny porcupines!

The podocarpus family includes 150 species. Many grow in **tropical** places. Most are tall trees with hard, yellowish wood. They are useful as timber. However, one podocarpus species is a **parasite.** Its **roots** penetrate another type of yellow wood and steal its water and **nutrients.** Some podocarpus conifer trees have broad leaves up to 14 inches (35 centimeters) long. They begin red and become greener as they grow older.

▲ The branches of a Chile pine tree form an umbrella shape at the top of a straight, patterned trunk.

Surprising sequoias
The giant sequoia (*Sequoiadendron giganteum*) of the western United States can reach amazing sizes. Some adult trees are 328 feet (100 meters) tall, measure 82 feet (25 meters) around, and have 20-inch-thick (50-centimeter-thick) bark and roots that spread 197 feet (60 meters) on all sides. They can weigh as much as 2,000 tons—the weight of ten blue whales!

What Are Flowering Plants?

The final division in the plant **kingdom**—flowering plants—is by far the largest. It contains **species** that look as different as beech trees and clover. These species are grouped together because they make flowers. The job of all flowers, large or small, is to make **seeds.**

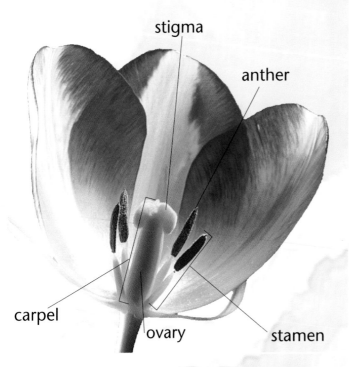

Using flowers to make seeds

Flowers contain male and female parts. Both make **sex cells.** Many kinds of plants have both male and female parts in the same flower. Some have separate male and female flowers on the same plant. Others have male and female flowers on separate plants. For a seed to begin to grow, a sex cell from a male part of a flower has to join with a sex cell from a female part.

▲ It is easy to spot the different parts of a flower in a tulip.

A flower's parts

The male parts of a flower are called **stamens.** The **anthers,** at the top of the stamens, produce the male sex cells, called **pollen.** The female parts of a flower are called the **carpel.** At the bottom of the carpel is the **ovary,** which contains the female sex cells. At the top of each carpel is a sticky pad called a **stigma.** If pollen lands on a stigma, it sticks there. Then the male sex cell can join with the female sex cell. This is called **fertilization.** The fertilized female sex cell develops into a seed.

◄ As this hummingbird collects nectar from a flower, its head is dusted with pollen. The pollen will rub off onto the next flower the bird visits.

Why do flowers look different?

The way a flower gets **pollinated** affects how it looks. Flowers that rely on animals such as insects for pollination have scents, colored **petals,** and **sepals.** These attract insects that come to eat the sugary **nectar** stored inside the flower. When insect visitors reach for a flower's nectar, they accidentally pick up pollen. When they visit another flower, the pollen is rubbed off onto the stigma.

Flowers that rely on wind for pollination tend to be much less colorful. They do not need bright colors, sweet scents, and food to attract insects. Their anthers and stigmas stick out from the flower so the wind can blow their pollen away.

From flower to fruit

As seeds develop, the ovary around them grows into a **fruit** and the other flower parts die. Fruits protect seeds and help move them to new ground, where they can **germinate.** The smell and taste of fleshy fruits attract animals. The animals eat the flesh and then spit out the seeds or deposit them in their droppings. Some flowering plants have fruit shaped like wings. They carry their seeds on the wind. Other flowering plants have fruits covered with tiny hooks. They catch onto an animal's fur and are moved to new ground.

Classifying Flowering Plants

Nine out of every ten **species** of plants on Earth are flowering plants. With such a variety of plants, scientists have come up with many ways to classify them.

▲ Flowers in the pea family have five petals and often look similar. This is a perennial pea (*Lathyrus latifolius*).

Features

Flowering plants can be grouped by their different features and characteristics. They can be sorted according to leaf shape. For instance, trees with five-pointed leaves belong to the maple family. Flowering plants also can be sorted by the shape or form of their flowers. For example, flowers that have a boat-shaped **petal**—which contains the **carpel** and **stamens**—and two roof petals are part of the pea family. Flowering trees can be grouped by the shape of their branches or by their different kinds of bark.

Life cycles

Flowering plants can also be divided according to their **life cycle.** Many are **annuals.** These plants make flowers and die in one growing season. Their **seeds germinate** the following year. Others are **biennials.** They grow and die in one season, but their **roots** survive the winter and fuel the growth of a new plant the following year. **Perennials** survive for many years without completely dying each year.

Monocots and dicots

One of the most important ways that scientists classify a flowering plant is by the number of **cotyledons** inside the plant's **seeds**. Cotyledons, also known as seed leaves, are food stores that help the **embryo** inside the seed to grow. Flowering plants have either one or two cotyledons inside each seed. If they have one cotyledon, they are called monocotyledons, or **monocots.** If they have two cotyledons, they are called dicotyledons, or **dicots.**

Because you usually cannot look inside a seed, there are other ways to tell monocots and dicots apart. In monocots, the **veins** are usually arranged in parallel lines along the length of the leaves. Tulips are monocots. In dicots, the leaves usually have one or several large veins with smaller ones branching off of them. Maple trees are dicots.

▼ **Monocots have parallel veins in their leaves. Dicots, such as this maple, have branched veins in their leaves.**

Types of Flowering Plants

Of the more than 250,000 **species** of flowering plants, about one-fifth are **monocots.** They include irises, onions, and lilies. The grass family of monocots is probably the most familiar to us. There are about 10,000 species in the grass family, including vital cereal crops such as wheat, rice, and corn; the hardy grasses that make sports fields; and bamboos so strong they are used to make buildings. Grasses are very quick-growing plants. They have tough but flexible **stems,** similar to their relatives, the rushes and sedges.

Awesome orchids

Orchids are another big family of monocots. There are nearly 20,000 species. Orchid flowers are very distinctive, with colorful, unusually shaped lower **petals.** Some orchids are **tropical** vines, such as the vanilla orchid. This plant's **seed pods** are used to flavor food. Many orchids are small plants that live in the soil in cold places. However, most are **epiphytes** in **rain forests.** These orchids grow on trees, so they are closer to the sun than they would be on the dark forest floor. Instead of growing underground, their **roots** hang in the humid air to absorb the moisture.

Exotic monocots

Some of the most familiar monocot trees include the coconut palm (*Cocos nucifera*) of tropical beaches and the date palms (*Phoenix dactylifera*) of hot deserts. The ginger family contains several important and familiar tropical monocot plants such as the banana (*Musa*), garden ginger (*Zingiber officinale*), and bird-of-paradise (*Strelitzia reginae*) flower.

▶ **These are flowers of the garden ginger plant.**

Dynamic dicots

The largest group of flowering plants are the **dicots.** About 190,000 species of flowering plants are dicots. This plant group contains a wide variety of plants, including the tiny wolffia duckweed, whose flowers are the size of the period at the end of this sentence. The group also includes the Australian eucalyptus tree, which reaches a height of 328 feet (100 meters).

The largest dicot families are the sunflowers and the peas. Most of the 24,000 members of the sunflower family have compound flowers. Their flower heads contain many small flowers, called florets. Some dicots, such as olive and coffee, are large trees or shrubs. Others, such as daisies, thistles, and chrysanthemums, are very small plants. The **legume** family contains such plants as beans, lentils, and groundnuts. They make their seeds in dry **fruits** called pods.

No family resemblance?

Scientists try to group plants based on how closely they are related—that is, how recently they shared a common **ancestor.** Sometimes they find close relationships between unlikely plants. The euphorbia family of dicots contains not only the poinsettia plants that are given as gifts in winter, but also cactus-like spurges. Both have special cup-shaped flowers that contain separate **anthers** and one or several **carpels** on a **stalk.**

▲ Waterlilies like this one are dicots. They grow and live in shallow water on the edges of ponds and lakes.

The Success of Flowering Plants

Flowering plants are found in almost every part of the planet, except the ocean. They live in **habitats** as different as windswept mountains, lush grasslands, marshes and bogs, dense forests, hot and cold deserts, and rushing rivers.

Adapt to survive

Some **species** of flowering plants can grow in several different habitats. However, most have **adapted** to life in one particular habitat. This means that over thousands or millions of years, the plants have changed and developed a shape, size, and **life cycle** ideally suited to the place where they grow. For example, cacti have adapted to life in hot, dry deserts. They have thick, fleshy **stems** that store water and thin, spiny leaves that help reduce the amount of water lost by **evaporation.**

▲ Flowering plants are so successful they even manage to live in some of the coldest places on Earth, such as Alaska.

Tree tactics

Trees have developed ways of surviving in their different habitats. In colder climates, **deciduous** trees drop their leaves in the fall so they are not damaged during the cold winter. New leaves grow in the spring. In monsoon climates, deciduous trees shed their leaves at the start of the dry season and grow new ones when the monsoon rains come. In countries with warm summers, cold winters, and light rain all year, some **evergreen** trees have no need to lose their leaves.

Plant partnerships

Flowering plants are so successful because they are able to use other **organisms** to help them grow and **reproduce.** For example, many flowering plants rely on particular animals for **pollination.** One orchid species has a long flower whose **nectar** and **pollen** can be reached only by a moth that has a 12-inch (30-centimeter) tongue. Each of the 1,000 different species of **tropical** fig tree needs a different wasp to pollinate its flowers.

Many flowering plants rely on **fungi** and **bacteria** in the places they grow. This is because fungi and bacteria help break down plants and animals that have died, releasing **nutrients.** Each tree species in the woods may rely on a massive underground **colony** of just one species of fungi to supply its nutrients.

Feeding off of others

Parasitic flowering plants, such as rafflesia, have **roots** that grow into other plants and steal the nutrients and food they need from them. **Carnivorous** plants, such as sundews, "eat" insects. They catch insects in trap- or tube-shaped leaves, then digest them using special juices.

▲ **This wasp is entering a fig fruit to lay its eggs.**

Fig nurseries

Figs and wasps help each other. Female wasps can pollinate fig flowers that are hidden inside what we think of as the **fruit,** but only if she lays her eggs on them. The fig then protects the growing wasps until they hatch and fly off.

Plants: Then and Now

We know that dinosaurs once lived on Earth because we have found **fossil** bones. We can imagine what their lives were like by studying these fossils and the dinosaur's close relatives of today—the lizards. Plant fossils give us similar clues about plants of the past.

Changing over time

Since the first plants appeared on Earth, continents have moved, oceans have become smaller, and temperatures have changed. Some plants could not survive these changes. They became extinct, or died out. Others survived because they were stronger in some way. These plants **reproduced,** and their offspring had the features that made their parents successful. Over millions of years, new plants developed. This is **evolution.** New **species** continue to evolve as **habitats** on Earth continue to change.

Like any kind of fossil, plant fossils cannot tell us everything about their past. Not everything that ever died on Earth has become a fossil. Some **organisms** simply rot away. However, if one plant fossil is in rock older than another plant fossil, it probably appeared on Earth first. From studying fossils, we know that the first plants, living in the sea thousands of millions of years ago, were very similar to today's algae.

▶ These are fossil horsetail plants that lived hundreds of millions of years ago. The horsetails of today look very similar to these ancient plants, but they are a lot smaller. Some early horsetails were 99 feet (30 meters) tall!

Plant evolution

As large areas of land emerged from the sea, some early plants washed ashore. Many died. But some survived in the drier conditions because they had thicker skins. Over time, mosses and liverworts evolved. These plants could live only in damp places because they reproduce by **spores** that **germinate** in water.

Other plants evolved into ferns and horsetails. They could grow taller, as they had **roots** and vessels to move water and food through their bodies. But they still needed moisture for spore germination. Much later, conifers evolved. Conifers reproduce using **seeds.** Seeds need less water to grow than spores do, so conifers spread to drier places. Conifers covered Earth 250 to 300 million years ago.

Later, flowering plants evolved. They used wind and the abundant insect life for **pollination.** Their developing seeds were protected and moved around by **fruits.** Each seed was packaged with the food it needed to germinate. These developments made reproduction in flowering plants rapid and successful. Today they are the most widespread plants on Earth.

Fossil records

The oldest plant fossils are of algae that lived 3.5 billion years ago. The earliest mosses appeared about 450 million years ago. Ferns, horsetails, and conifers all appeared by 250 to 300 million years ago. The first flowering plants appeared about 150 million years later.

◄ This is a fossil of an early flower, found in Wyoming.

Studying Plants

In the past, plant scientists—called botanists—studied plants by picking those that looked interesting or rare and then taking them home for study. There were many problems with this. To begin, the botanists killed the plants, which often rotted before they could be studied. And, once the botanists took the plants from where they grew, they could not see how the plants fit into their **habitats.**

Today we know it's better to look at, write notes about, draw, or photograph plants in their habitats. We can then compare and confirm this information using specimens kept in museums or special gardens. If botanists today need to collect a specimen to study it, they have better means of keeping it fresh than they did in the past. They can travel much more quickly and easily.

▲ It is still easier to pick rare orchids than it is to grow them. That's why many species, including this orchid, *Butea frondosa*, have become **endangered.**

The orchid hunters

Orchids became so popular about 250 years ago that rich people hired professional orchid hunters to find new types. The hunters risked death from snake bites, disease, and falls from trees as they tried to reach unusual **epiphyte** varieties many feet above ground in tropical rain forests. Some types became so prized that they were sold for hundreds of thousands of dollars!

Has plant collecting helped us?

Plant collectors have changed the way people look and how they feed and cure themselves. European collectors brought back rhododendrons from Asia to fill their gardens, and potatoes from South America to fill their stomachs. Much European and American wealth came from the sale of sugar, cocoa, spices, and cotton crops grown and tended by slaves in **tropical** countries. Plant medicines used by local people in tropical countries have been collected and used worldwide.

Counting on classification

Although hundreds of thousands of plant **species** have been identified, some botanists believe that many thousands more are waiting to be found in the lush tropical **rain forests.** By classifying plants, we not only identify the different species we already know and figure out how they may have evolved, we also recognize new species. Some of these may be useful to us.

By protecting and studying plants and how they live in their habitats, we can better understand how the lives of all living things on Earth are connected. Classification can then benefit not only those on Earth now, but also future generations who will live here.

▶ In remote parts of the world's rain forests, there may be plants yet to be discovered that will cure diseases such as cancer.

Try It Yourself!

Classification practice

Classification is all about sorting and grouping. You can classify just about anything, but it is good to start with a simple exercise.

You will need:
- large sheet of butcher paper
- pencil or pen
- 8 different small objects (button, shell, stone, pencil, eraser, etc.)

Lay the paper lengthwise on a table. Draw a big circle at the top middle of the paper. Next draw two arrows leading to two smaller circles below the big circle. Then draw two arrows and two smaller circles below each of those circles. Repeat this process until you have eight circles in a row.

Place the eight objects into the big circle at the top. Divide the objects into two groups in different ways: by size (large or small) or whether they were found or bought, for example. Make a note of how you divided them. Place the two groups of objects into the two smaller circles. Then subdivide each group into two smaller groups. Divide them in a different way than you did before. For instance, divide them by color or by shape. Again, note how you divided them.

Repeat this process until you have each object in its own circle. You should also, by now, have a list of the different ways you divided the objects at each step.

Now repeat this process. But this time, mix up the different ways of dividing the objects and see if you end up with the same groups. Often you will not, and this shows how tricky classification can be!

This exercise is similar to the way plants are classified. The smallest circles are like **species** names, the next largest circles are like **genus** names, and so on.

Scientists don't just use shape, size, and color to classify plants. They use leaf and flower shape, arrangements of leaves on branches, whether a plant makes **seeds** or **spores,** and many other different characteristics.

Monocot or dicot?

Flowering plants are usually divided into two groups depending on whether they have

- one or two seed leaves (food stores), called **cotyledons,** inside their seeds
- parallel (side-by-side) **veins** or veins in a branched arrangement in their leaves.

Try to classify **monocots** and **dicots** yourself.

You will need:

- roasted peanuts in shells
- small can of sweet corn
- grass seeds
- watercress seeds
- 2 plates
- 2 circles of blotting paper
- 2 clear plastic pots that fit over the plates
- magnifying glass

One or two parts?

Break open some peanut shells, rub off the brown skins, and examine the peanuts. These are dicots. The two cotyledons are the two halves of each peanut.

Ask an adult to open the can of sweet corn. Examine some of the corn kernels. Pinch off the yellow seed coat. A corn seed is a monocot. It is in one piece.

One or two seed leaves?

Place each piece of paper onto one saucer and moisten the paper with water. Sprinkle watercress seeds on one and grass seeds on the other. Put a plastic pot over the top of each plate. Then carefully place the plates in a sunny place, out of the way, perhaps on a windowsill. When the seeds have **germinated,** look at the leaves that first come out of the seed cases with the magnifying glass.

Watercress is a dicot, so you should see two mini-leaves emerge from the watercress seeds. Grass is a monocot. You should see only one leaf emerging from each grass seed.

Looking at Plant Classification

The plant **kingdom** is usually divided into five divisions. Most plants make their own food by **photosynthesis,** using a green chemical called **chlorophyll.** This causes most plants to look green. However, some plants contain other chemicals that mask the chlorophyll and make them look a different color.

Classification is tricky, and not everyone agrees on a single system. For example, because algae are different from most other plants, some scientists classify them in a kingdom called Protista, which also contains microscopic **organisms** that can move in water.

Algae:
- range in size from simple single **cells** or short chains of cells to more complex giant seaweeds.
- live in water or very damp places; most live in seawater.
- are **nonvascular.**
- **reproduce** using **spores** made in swellings on leaf-like **fronds.**
- have no **roots;** many have **holdfasts** to anchor themselves.
- are a food source of marine food chains.

There are about 12,000 **species** of algae. They are divided into three groups within the algae division: red algae, green algae, and brown algae.

Mosses and liverworts:
- are small, green land plants that often grow in **colonies.**
- usually live in damp places, from bogs to soil to tree bark
- are nonvascular.
- reproduce using spores made in **capsules.**
- have root-like rhizoids to anchor them.

There are about 24,000 species of mosses and liverworts.

Ferns, horsetails, and club mosses:

- are green land plants that vary in size.
- are **vascular.**
- reproduce using spores that are made in cases called **sporangia** on the undersides of fronds in ferns, at the ends of **stems** in horsetails, and on special groups of leaves in club mosses.
- have large frond-like fern leaves that unwind and expand as they grow.
- typically spread using underground stems (**rhizomes**).

There are about 12,500 species of ferns, horsetails, and club mosses.

Conifers:

- vary in size, from small shrubs to enormous trees.
- usually have needlelike leaves and are usually **evergreen.**
- are vascular.
- reproduce using **seeds** made in **cones.**
- have two types of cones.
- reproduce when wind carries **pollen** from male cone to female cone, where a seed develops from a **fertilized ovule.**

There are 500 species of conifers, divided into three groups: conifers, cycads, and ginkgoes.

Flowering plants:

- vary immensely in size and in form.
- are the dominant vegetation on Earth, growing in most **habitats.**
- usually have well-defined leaves, stems, and roots.
- are vascular, with complex **xylem** and **phloem** tissue.
- reproduce using seeds made in flowers.
- have flowers with male **stamens** and female **carpels**; the pollen is carried from stamens to carpels by animal **pollinators**, wind, or water.
- have seeds that develop inside **fruit.**

There are about 250,000 species of flowering plants, divided into two groups: **monocots** and **dicots.**

Glossary

adapt change over thousands or millions of years to fit in with a habitat

ancestor earlier generation of organisms. For example, your great-grandparents and your grandparents are your ancestors.

annual plant that grows, flowers, makes seeds, and dies all within one year or season

anther top part of the male part of a flower, or stamen, where pollen is found in pollen sacs

bacteria tiny organisms in the soil, water, and air

biennial plant that lives for two years. It usually flowers, makes seeds, and dies in the second year.

capsule container of spores found at the end of stalks on certain plants

carbon dioxide gas in the air that plants use for photosynthesis

carnivorous plant or animal that eats parts of insects or other animals

carpel name for the female parts of a flower. The ovary, style, and stigma together make up a carpel.

cell building block of living things

chlorophyll green substance found in plants that is used in photosynthesis

colony/colonies group of similar plants that take over an area of land

cone form of dry fruit, in which seeds develop, produced by conifer trees

consumer organism that needs to consume, or eat, plants or animals that eat plants in order to live

cotyledon food store that helps the embryo inside the seed to grow

deciduous trees that lose all their leaves at about the same time

dicot type of plant that has two seed leaves, called cotyledons, inside each of its seeds

drought long period without rain

embryo very young plant contained in a seed

endangered describes a plant or animal in danger of dying out

energy ability in living things to do what they need to in order to carry out life processes

epiphyte plant that grows on another plant for support

evaporation when water turns from liquid into a vapor, or gas

evergreen plant that does not lose all its leaves at once, but loses some and grows new ones all year long

evolution way new kinds of plants and animals come into being as a result of many small changes that happen over thousands or millions of years

fertilize/fertilization when a male sex cell and a female sex cell join together and begin to form a seed

fossil preserved remains of a plant or animal that lived millions of years ago

frond leaflike part of a plant, such as a fern or seaweed

fruit part of a plant that contains and protects its seeds

fungi group of living things that cannot make their own food by photosynthesis. Mushrooms are fungi.

gene set of instructions that control how an organism looks and how it will survive, grow, and change through its life

genus in Linnaeus's double name system, a general, or group, name

germinate/germination when a seed starts to grow

habitat place where plants or animals live

holdfast rootlike part of a plant, such as seaweed, that the plants uses to hold onto a rock. Holdfasts are not roots.

kingdom in classification, the largest group that living things belong to

legume family of plants that all grow their seeds inside pods. Peas and beans are legumes.

life cycle order of events in the life of an organism

monocot type of plant that has one seed leaf inside each seed

nectar sugary liquid plants make to attract insects

nonvascular plants that do not have tubes for transporting fluids

nutrient kind of chemical that nourishes plants and animals, keeping them healthy

organism living thing, such as a bacterium, cell, plant, or animal

ovary rounded bottom part of the carpel that contains the female sex cell.

ovule plant's female sex cell

oxygen gas in the air and gas that plants release into the air during the process of photosynthesis

parasite/parasitic plant or animal that lives on and gets its food from another living thing

peat partly rotted remains of plants

perennial plant that lives for more than two years, often for many years

petal usually the largest and most colorful part of a flower

phloem tubes that carry food made in the leaf to other parts of the plant

photosynthesis process by which plants make their own food using water, carbon dioxide, and energy from sunlight

plankton microscopic organisms that live in the surface waters of the ocean

pod capsule that holds the seeds of legume plants such as peas

pollen tiny, dustlike particles produced by a flower that contain the plant's male sex cells

pollinate/pollination when pollen travels from the anthers of one flower to the stigma of the same or a different flower.

pollinator insect or animal that carries pollen from one flower to another

pollution poisons or other harmful substances found in any part of the environment

producer organism that produces its own food within itself

prothallus tiny plantlike organism that grows from a spore. A fern prothallus can produce a new fern plant.

rain forest type of forest that exists in very hot and rainy countries of the world

reproduce/reproduction when a living thing produces young like itself.

resin sticky sap that flows just beneath a tree's layer of bark.

rhizome kind of stem that grows underground instead of up in the air

root plant part that anchors a plant firmly in the ground and takes in water and nutrients

sap sugary fluid containing food made in the leaves. Sap flows in a plant's phloem tubes.

seed part of the plant that contains the beginnings of a new plant

sepal green petal-like structure. Sepals protect the inner parts of a bud until the bud is ready to open.

sex cells cells that allow plants to reproduce

species group of living things that are similar in many ways and can reproduce together

sporangia sac or capsule containing groups of spores

spore tiny particle, usually containing a single cell, that can grow into a new plant

stalks part of the plant that attaches the leaf to the stem

stamen male reproductive part of a flower that produces pollen

stem part of the plant that holds it upright and supports its leaves and flowers

stigma part of the flower that receives pollen in the process of pollination. Stigmas are usually found at the top of a stalk.

timber wood that has been cut from a tree to be used for building or making furniture

tropical area of the world around the equator, which has the hottest climate on Earth

tundra name for areas in the Arctic regions of the world that are free from snow and ice for only a few months of the year.

vascular plants that have xylem and phloem tubes for transporting water, nutrients, and food to the various plant parts

vein tiny tube that supports a leaf. Xylem and phloem tubes run through the veins, carrying water and food around the plant.

xylem tube in a plant that carries water and nutrients from the roots to the other parts of the plant

Find Out More

Books

Bailey, Jill. *Plants and Plant Life*. Danbury, Conn.: Grolier Educational, 2000.

Burnie, David. *The Plant*. New York: Dorling Kindersley, 2000.

Dorling Kindersley Publishing Staff. *Extraordinary Plants*. New York: Dorling Kindersley, 1997.

Joly, Dominique, et al. *How Does Your Garden Grow? Be Your Own Plant Expert*. New York: Sterling Publishing Company, 2000.

Madgwick, Wendy. *Flowering Plants: The Green World*. Collingdale, Penn.: DIANE Publishing Company, 2000.

Oxlade, Chris. *Flowering Plants*. Danbury, Conn.: Children's Press, 1999.

Conservation sites

Center for Plant Conservation
P.O. Box 299
St. Louis, MO 63166-0299
Tel: (314) 577-9450

Lady Bird Johnson Wildflower Center
4801 La Crosse Avenue
Austin, TX 78739-1702
Tel: (512) 292-4200

New England Wild Flower Society
180 Hemenway Road
Framingham, MA 01701
Tel: (508) 877-7630

California Native Plant Society
1722 J Street, Suite 17
Sacramento, CA 95814
Tel: (415) 970-0394

The State Botanical Garden of Georgia
2450 S. Milledge Avenue
Athens, GA 30605
Tel: (706) 542-6448

Places to visit

Many museums, arboretums (botanical gardens devoted to trees), and botanic gardens are fascinating places to visit. You could try:

The New York Botanical Garden
Bronx River Parkway at Fordham Road
Bronx, NY 10458
Tel: (718) 817-8700

Denver Botanic Gardens
1005 York Street
Denver, CO 80206
Tel: (720) 865-3500

Atlanta Botanical Garden
1345 Piedmont Avenue NE
Atlanta, GA 30309
Tel: (404) 876-5859

Garfield Park Conservatory
300 North Central Park Ave.
Chicago, IL 60624-1996
Tel: (312) 746-5100

University of California Botanical Garden
200 Centennial Drive
Berkeley, CA 94720
Tel: (510) 643-2755

Missouri Botanical Garden
P.O. Box 299
St. Louis, MO 63166-0299
Tel: (314) 577-9400

Index